D1644519

CITY CYCLING
BARCELONA

Rapha.

Thames & Hudson

Created by Andrew Edwards and Max Leonard of
Tandem London, a design, print and editorial studio

Thanks to Judy Kaufmann for illustrations;
Marta Puigdemasa, Perdiz Magazine and Leo Tong
for city spots; and Dave Corkle for racing, training
and wrenching advice

First published in the United Kingdom in 2013 by
Thames & Hudson Ltd, 181A High Holborn, London WC1V 7QX

City Cycling Barcelona © 2013 Andrew Edwards and Max Leonard
Illustrations © 2013 Thames & Hudson Ltd, London and Rapha Racing Ltd

Designed by Andrew Edwards

Illustrations © 2013 Judy Kaufmann, judykaufmann.com

British Library Cataloguing-in-Publication Data
A catalogue record for this book is available from the British Library

ISBN 978-0-500-29106-1

Printed and bound in China by Everbest Printing Co Ltd

To find out about all our publications, please visit
www.thamesandhudson.com. There you can subscribe
to our e-newsletter, browse or download our current catalogue,
and buy any titles that are in print.

CONTENTS

HOW TO USE THIS GUIDE

This Barcelona volume of the *City Cycling* series is designed to give you the confidence to explore the city by bike at your own pace. On the front flaps is a locator map of the whole city to help you orient yourself. We've divided the city up into four different neighbourhoods: El Raval (p. 10); Montjuïc (p. 16); Gràcia and L'Eixample (p. 22); and Poblenou (p. 30). All are easily accessible by bike, and are full of cafés, bars, galleries, museums, shops and parks. Each area is mapped in detail, and our recommendations for places of interest and where to fuel up on coffee and cake, as well as where to find a Wi-Fi connection, are marked. Take a pootle round on your bike and see what suits you.

The neighbourhood maps also show bike routes, bike shops and landmarks – everything you need to navigate safely and pinpoint specific locations across a large section of the centre of town. If you fancy a set itinerary, turn to A Day On The Bike, also on the front flaps. It takes you on a relaxed 30km (18-mile) route through some of the parts of Barcelona we haven't featured in the neighbourhood sections, and visits a few of the more touristy sights. Pick and choose the bits you fancy, go from back to front, and use the route as it suits you.

A section on Racing and Training (p. 36) fills you in on some of Barcelona's cycling heritage, and provides ideas for longer rides if you want to explore the beautiful countryside around the city, while Essential Bike Info (p. 40) discusses road etiquette and the ins and outs of navigating your way along Barcelona's cycle routes. Finally, Links and Addresses (p. 44) will give you the practical details you need to know.

BARCELONA:
THE CYCLING CITY

If your idea of fun on a bike is beach cruising, then – of all the major cities in Europe – Barcelona is the place for you. Add in Picasso (there is a museum dedicated to the artist), Gaudí (whose magnum opus, Sagrada Família, is here) and stunning modern architecture, as well as an unlimited choice of bars and restaurants at which to while the night away, all in a compact and friendly city centre, and Barcelona by bike becomes irresistible. It's a vibrant place, and the warm climate is conducive to cycling almost all year round – it's why a lot of professional cyclists live in nearby Girona, which has even better access to mountain roads than the Catalan capital.

Not that we expect our city cyclists to be racing around under the Mediterranean sun: far better to pedal lazily under the palm trees from one cool drink to another, so as not to break too much of a sweat. And more than any other city in the *City Cycling Europe* series, Barcelona is a place to cycle at night. In the summer, the city is quiet in the morning (meaning you can have the cool early hours gloriously to yourself if you choose), and people often spend the hottest part of the day (in the late afternoon) out of sight, so the place really comes to life late in the evening, when you may find yourself cycling to a tapas restaurant or a flamenco bar, or down along the beach.

While it doesn't have a strong historic bike culture, Barcelona has never ceded its public spaces to the motor car. It is the third-densest European city after Paris and Athens, and much of the population live in car-free streets and walk for transport. In large portions of the *ciutat vella* pedestrians monopolize the streets, as cars are either prohibited completely or only allowed in at certain times. And while the sinuous paths of the Barri Gòtic, in particular, can be confusing to navigate, they're entirely safe and pleasant to cycle around. Even outside the historic centre of town, there is relatively little on-street parking, an effective disincentive for car use, and a good network of cycle lanes on Barcelona's larger roads. A recent pivotal moment for cycling in the city was the introduction of the Bicing bike-sharing scheme. That was in 2007; in that year alone, the number of people cycling each day jumped by 81 per cent, and the number of people who cycle regularly has continued to increase.

The Bicing scheme is considered a great success, but it's not open to non-residents, so you'll have to make do with a commercial rental bike (for more about the Bicing debate, and where to find a good rental, turn to the Essential Bike Info section [p. 40]). Luckily, there are lots of places to hire bikes in Barcelona; pick one up and escape the old town and city centre by cycling along the seafront with the wind in your hair. Or pedal out along the wide, straight boulevards of L'Eixample, and you'll find most of the city is within easy reach. Although some of the roads in the grid system are fast and full of traffic, there's always a cycle lane somewhere near. By tic-tacking your way across the grid, you can cover large distances quite quickly, and it's far better than sitting on the Metro or on a bus.

Along the seafront, and in most of L'Eixample, the terrain is gloriously flat, but it's an inescapable fact that the city is surrounded by mountains – the cable car and the hills on the horizon are a dead giveaway. Gràcia slopes up to the northwest, and Montjuïc puts an abrupt stop to the city in the south. But these hills are nothing to be feared – indeed, many racing cyclists relish them! Take your time and don't force the pace, and you'll find the ride up to the Castell de Montjuïc (p. 17), say, or to Park Güell – where you'll see sightseers being disgorged from hot coaches – extremely satisfying. Don't lose heart, and remember you can always stop for a drink and an ice cream … and just think about freewheeling back down again afterwards.

NEIGHBOURHOODS

EL RAVAL

THE CITY'S BEATING HEART

El Raval is one side of Barcelona's old town. The other, just across <u>La Rambla</u>, is Barri Gòtic, the dense labyrinth of medieval streets and small squares. Although picturesque, it's difficult to successfully nav igate on a bike: the crowds and narrow serpentine passages make for tough going. El Raval, however, is a bit more open, a bit less crowded and equally as vibrant. You'll find bars, cafés and historical buildings – a pulsating, culture-filled, alcohol-fuelled neighbourhood as full of daylife and nightlife as Gòtic (and with fewer lowlifes).

Let's say you're coming at El Raval from La Rambla, where you can duck into **Arts Santa Mònica** ①, an innovative cultural space.

Here, you might see an art installation or an exhibition of war-zone relics collected by a photojournalist, or attend a poetry event. Head into the maze of streets – it's no embarrassment to have to keep checking your map – and you'll pass **Bar Pastís** ② (no prizes for guessing the speciality) and **Miscelänea** ③, a small gallery, bar and shop where there's always something happening. **Marsella** ④, another French-themed bar, is also one of our evening picks, but there are a lot of places on the <u>Rambla del Raval</u> to choose from, including the **Hotel Barceló Raval** ⑤, a shimmering piece of architecture with a panoramic rooftop bar and a *Twin Peaks*-inspired lobby. As you cycle along the shaded Rambla, watch out for *El Gato del Raval* ⑥, Fernando Botero's protuberant statue. Also close is the **Filmoteca de Catalunya** ⑦, of interest to visitors mainly for Josep Lluís Mateo's building. Further north, **Grey Street** ⑧ is a local art and crafts shop that happens to surround **Satan's Coffee Corner**, a little hole-in-the-wall place serving some of the city's best coffee.

In this central part of the neighbourhood, above the hive of student activity in the picturesque old buildings around the <u>Carrer Hospital</u>, are two of the city's heavyweight cultural institutions. **CCCB** ⑨ is the Centre of Contemporary Culture, which hosts an acclaimed eclectic programme of events focusing on urban life and cities. Just next to it, in a square reverberating with the sound of skateboarders, is one of Barcelona's most emblematic buildings, **MACBA** ⑩, the museum of contemporary art. **Fàbrica Moritz** ⑪, meanwhile, is a new cultural space in the former Moritz brewery. The additions are designed by Jean Nouvel, and there's a lush vertical garden by Patrick Blanc. Don't head over, though, without exploring behind the museum, where the streets are full of shops and bars.

Luchador Records ⑫ and **Discos Paradiso** ⑬ are two of the city's best record shops, **Chandal** ⑭ is full of gadgets and design knick-knacks, and **Llibreria La Central del Raval** ⑮ is a place to lose yourself among books and magazines for an hour or two. If it's sunny, **Wilde Vintage** ⑯, which sells only vintage sunglasses, could be useful. They'll also come in handy at **Dos Palillos** ⑰, an in-vogue tapas/Asian fusion restaurant that's part of **Casa Camper**, one of Barcelona's original boutique hotels – cyclists staying here can borrow any of the bikes hanging from the ceiling in the lobby. For late-night eats, **Bohèmic** ⑱ serves some of the best tapas in town.

REFUELLING

FOOD	DRINK
Caravelle ⑲ is a must for brunch, coffee and inventive lunches	**Olivia Café** ㉑ is a good coffee stop
Sésamo ⑳ makes good vegetarian food	**Betty Ford** ㉒ is a raucous cocktail bar that also does good beer and burgers

WI-FI
Lletraferit ㉓, a bookshop and café, also has Wi-Fi

MONTJUÏC

PARKS, ARCHITECTURE AND GRAND VIEWS

If you remember the Barcelona Olympics, you'll remember the scene: a diver perched at an impossible height on the 10m (33 ft) board, with the city spread out beneath him. That was on Montjuïc, and the diving pool – or **Piscina Municipal de Montjuïc** ① – still survives (albeit in a sadly dilapidated state), along with much of the Games' architecture and facilities. Montjuïc, looming over the Poble Sec and Montjuïc-Sants neighbourhoods, is a short cycle southwest from the city centre. Along with the Olympics relics on the top of the hill, there are also world-class museums and glorious parkland, and it's worth gritting your teeth and riding your bike all the way up for the views.

The summit is 185m (607 ft) above sea level and, given you probably started near the beach, getting to the top is no small achievement. It's also satisfying to know that 'ordinary' tourists probably caught the cable car, which drops them at the largely seventeenth-century **Castell de Montjuïc** ②, a fortress that often doubled up as a prison, even into the Franco regime. It offers a beautiful vantage point over the city and to the south over the docks, and the surrounding paths and trails offer easy and scenic off-road riding – you're really in the middle of nature up here. Ride round far enough and you'll reach the **Caseta del Migdia** ③, a chilled-out open-air café at the Mirador del Migdia, with views over Barcelona.

Stop here for *barbacoa* and refreshments in the shade. Running down the side of the hill is the **Jardí Botànic** ④, with its eye-catching triangular structures of walkways and plants, and the **Estadi Olímpic Lluís Companys** ⑤. Built for the 1929 International Expo, it formed part of Barcelona's bid for the Olympics in 1936. Although the Games went to Berlin, the stadium got its chance to star, many years later, as the main arena for the 1992 Olympics. More noticeable is the **Montjuïc Communications Tower** ⑥, designed by Santiago Calatrava in 1992, which appears to swoop down over the city. Tucked underneath is the **Museu Olímpic i de l'Esport Joan Antoni Samaranch** ⑦, a museum dedicated to sport, and further down are the **Fundació Joan Miró** ⑧, dedicated to the Catalan artist, and another art museum, the **CaixaForum** ⑨.

Freewheel back down the hill towards them, and pretend you're in San Francisco – the plantlife and scenery aren't much different. If you glance over your left shoulder, you may spy the foreboding **Cementiri de Montjuïc** ⑩, where Miró is buried. Don't leave the broad sweeps of the hill road without stopping at the grand Palau Nacional, another relic of the 1929 Expo, which now houses **MNAC**

⑪, the national museum of Catalan art. In its grounds is the **Pavelló Mies van der Rohe** ⑫. Designed by the Bauhaus luminary, the perfect, simple pavilion is made from four types of marble and was restored in the 1980s. Inside are examples of Mies's 'Barcelona' chair, and there's a sculpture by Georg Kolbe in the courtyard. Below the Palau Nacional, buildings start to crowd in and you know you're in civilization again. You'll pass dance and performance venue **Mercat de les Flors** ⑬ and, in Poble Sec proper, **Tinto Roja** ⑭, a tango bar in a former cabaret, as well as **Los Juanele** ⑮, an authentic flamenco bar beloved of locals. That doesn't get going until the early hours; beforehand, try **Quimet & Quimet** ⑯, a top-quality tapas bar.

REFUELLING

FOOD

La Tomaquera ⑰ is always busy with locals wanting Catalan cooking

DRINK

La Fibula ⑱ is a Middle Eastern-style teahouse with baklava, too

Zodiaco ⑲ – good for drinks after dark

WI-FI

Bar Seco ⑳ has a nice patio, microbrewery beers, Catalan and veggie food, and free Wi-Fi

GRÀCIA & L'EIXAMPLE

CLASSY SHOPPING AND A VILLAGE WITHIN THE CITY

When Barcelona expanded in the nineteenth century, town planner Ildefons Cerdà's vision was of long boulevards and light, airy cross-roads, with a characteristic octagonal design. It's all still there in L'Eixample (Catalan for 'extension'). Today, some of the boulevards are at the mercy of car traffic, but it still retains the ease of living and all the markets and amenities he envisaged. Gràcia, to the north, above the Avinguda Diagonal, did not welcome the advancing city: it did not become absorbed into Barcelona until 1897 and, like wider Catalonia, remains fiercely independent in spirit. The *barri* is still very much its own place and has a village-like feel, populated with a mix

of locals, arty types and international drifters, and its small streets and communal squares are home to plenty of shops, bars and restaurants.

If you're heading there from the centre of town, take the shady and tree-lined <u>Rambla de Catalunya</u>, where you'll be surrounded by cafés and terraces, rather than the busier <u>Passeig de Gràcia</u> (our Day On The Bike route explores its Gaudí and *Modernisme* treats). This part of L'Eixample is home to the **Fundació Antoni Tàpies** ①, a centre for artistic study set up by the Catalan artist and home to an impressive collection of modern art. There's also **Kowasa** ②, Spain's most famous photography gallery, with a correspondingly

good bookshop. **L'Appartement** ③ sells designer bits, but the real design treasure of the area is **Vinçon** ④, which features everything from furniture to stationery, bathroom wares, crockery and textiles, all under one roof. Around the Passeig de Gràcia, meanwhile, cluster Barcelona's crop of high-fashion boutiques. Leave behind the international names and search out **Santa Eulalia** ⑤ for men's and women's styles, or **The Outpost** ⑥ for men's shoes and accessories. To get away from the glad rags completely, the **Mercat de la Concepció** ⑦ is a flower market that's open twenty-four hours a day. It does fruit and vegetables, too.

Head north from Diagonal, and when the streets close in and you see the Catalan flag flying from balconies everywhere, you know you're in Gràcia. Head to <u>Plaça del Sol</u>, one of the area's most laid-back squares, for tapas at **Sol Soler** ⑧, or to <u>Plaça de la Revolución</u> for ice cream from **Gelateria Italiana** ⑨. If you have deep pockets, **Botafumeiro** ⑩ is one of the city's best and most prestigious seafood restaurants. For boutiques, cheap eats and antiques (at **Alzira** ⑪) <u>Carrer Verdi</u> is good for a relaxed pedal or even a stroll, while <u>Carrer de Torrijos</u> and <u>Travessera di Gràcia</u> are also good for a rummage owing to the numerous small boutiques promoting young designers. And **Duduá** ⑫, close by, is a shop and workshop showcasing textiles and crafts from young Barcelonans.

In the evening, stay in Gràcia for live music and a good atmosphere at **Heliogàbal** ⑬, or try cycling-themed bars **El Ciclista** ⑭ or **El Velódromo** ⑮ (which is also good for tapas, or a breakfast coffee and pastry). More upmarket are the wine bars **Viblioteca** ⑯ and L'Eixample's **Monvínic** ⑰; for cocktails in the grand old style, head to **Belvedere** ⑱, located in a house on an avenue lined with orange and lemon trees.

REFUELLING

FOOD	DRINK
Ikastola ⑲ has the best *bocatas* (sandwiches) in town	**Cosmo** ㉑, a cosy café/art gallery in L'Eixample
Churrería El Trébol ⑳ for *churros*, a sweet snack	**Bobby Gin** ㉒, if you're on a quest for the perfect gin and tonic

WI-FI

La Fourmi ㉓ is a café that offers vintage furniture, Fritz Lang posters and free Wi-Fi – open from breakfast-time all day

POBLENOU

DUSTY STREETS, LATE-NIGHT TREATS,
MODERN ARCHITECTURE

As Barcelona's textile industry declined between the 1960s and the '90s, Poblenou lost more than a thousand factories, leaving it something of a ghost town. Today, it has been rejuvenated by an influx of artists, small businesses and designers keen for space. It still feels quiet (but it sure wakes up at night!) and, on hot afternoons, in the dusty streets with their auto shops and warehouses, you feel as if you could be in Texas. It was the 1992 Olympics that really jump-started the area's rebirth (**Port Olímpic** ①, which hosted the sailing events, is at its western edge) – most importantly by removing the railway tracks that separated the neighbourhood from the sea – and now its beaches, including **Bogatell** ②, are some of the nicest in the city.

Since 1992, some daring architectural projects have given Poblenou new character, and a high-tech regeneration scheme, the '22@' plan, is masterminding its transformation into a digital hub. The most visible sign of changing fortunes is the **Torre Agbar** ③, which dominates the skyline. The Jean Nouvel-designed tower will remind Londoners of their own Swiss Re building (designed by Norman Foster, though the Torre Agbar is far more colourful at night), and others of … all sorts of things. Colourful local nicknames abound. At its foot, the **Els Encants flea market** ④ is the bastard love child of an antiques shop in London and a car-boot sale in Kabul. Pick your way through the broken TV sets and dirty silverware, battered books

and wooden picture frames, and you may find some bargains. The
<u>Carrer Dos de Maig</u> has several interesting bric-à-brac shops, too.

Also by Jean Nouvel – here as 'parkitecht', perhaps – is the **Parc
del Centre del Poblenou** ⑤, which is full of surprising sculptures,
while the landscaped grounds of the **Parc de la Diagonal Mar** ⑥
contain swooping paths and metalwork. The **Museu Blau** ⑦, a huge,
squat diamond on the seafront, designed by Herzog & de Meuron,
contains the natural history museum, and on a smaller scale, Jordi
Badia's concrete museum building for **Can Framis** ⑧ holds a collection of contemporary Catalan art. Nearby the **Barcelona Digital
Centro Tecnológico** ⑨ is an eye-catching, hyper-modern building
that houses tech start-ups. **Niu BCN** ⑩ is another good indication
of what's going on: it's a small performance space, with an emphasis
on digital creativity. There are also prestigious designers at work in
Poblenou. Mariscal, creator of the identity for the 1992 Olympics, is
based in the **Fundaçio Palo Alto** ⑪, a creative complex in a former
fabrics factory, set in lush gardens. You can join them for lunch in
the Cantina Palo Alto. **BD Barcelona Design** ⑫, the city's most
famous furniture and interior design studio, also keeps a showroom
in the neighbourhood.

It's not all hi-tech and fast moving, though. On **La Rambla de Poblenou** ⑬, the heart of the old quarter, life is as tranquil as it is busy on La Rambla in the city centre. The <u>Carrer Enric Granados</u>, too, makes for a relaxing cycle, and the **Cementiri de Poblenou** ⑭, with its amazing monuments and grave architecture, is dead quiet! As the sun goes down, **L'Ovella Negra** ⑮ is good for a beer, while **Razzmatazz** ⑯ is the established place for live music and late-night drinking – start the night here to find out about the more underground parties in this happening neighbourhood. **Els Pescadors** ⑰, on the other hand, is in a beautiful whitewashed square and is renowned for some of the freshest seafood in town.

REFUELLING

FOOD	DRINK
La Taqueria ⑱, near Gaudí's Sagrada Família, will plug a hole	**Chiringuito Inercia** ⑲ does classic cocktails on Nova Icària beach

WI-FI
Chiringuito Mochima ⑳ on Mar Bella beach is the perfect place to relax and connect to the free municipal Wi-Fi

RACING AND TRAINING

Girona, about 100km (62 miles) from Barcelona, is the town best known for road cycling in Catalonia, thanks to the pros that followed Lance Armstrong there in the early 2000s. Today there's still an impressive colony of international professionals, attracted by the decent year-round weather and the foothills of the Pyrenees, just visible on the horizon. It's close enough to the city for an overnight trip to pit yourself against climbs such as the **Rocacorba**, beloved of David Millar, but for non-pros, the hills within the city limits pose challenge enough. There's an amazing variety of climbs and, since the hills have kept Barcelona's spread in check, nice roads are just a stone's throw away. Try, for instance, the Tibidabo mountain. It's recognizable from far and wide thanks to the distinctive **Sagrat Cor** church on its ridge, and the **Torre de Collserola**, a communications tower built by Foster + Partners for the 1992 Olympics. Strike out for it on <u>Carretera de les Aigües</u>, and stop for a drink at **Mirablau** when you get thirsty.

For a longer ride, head off up <u>Carretera Cerdanyola-Horta</u>; or try the <u>N2</u>, which runs north up the coast and is a popular winter run. <u>Carretera de l'Arrabassada</u> to St Cugat del Vallès also sees heavy cyclist traffic, and <u>Carretera de la Roca</u>, which follows the Besòs river, is another good bet. If you want a group ride with local cyclists, **Galvesport** is a road-bike shop with rides up to 60 fast kilometres (37 miles), leaving from its door every day at 2pm. Also try **CC Gràcia**, a local cycling club that rides every Saturday morning at 8:30 from **Els Jardinets de Gràcia** on <u>Passeig de Gràcia</u>, just above Avinguda Diagonal. From February to November, they split into groups, depending on ability – whether a 120km (75 miles) fast ride with the hitters or a pootle along the coast, you'll find your level here. Alternatively, **EC Sant Andreu** club rides from **Estació de Sant Andreu Arenal** every Saturday at 7:30 (later in the winter), also dividing into groups. If these don't suit, a friendly bike shop will likely point you in the right direction. For more route ideas, check the Links and Addresses section.

For road-bike spares and repairs, Galvesport (see above) is a good traditional shop run by an ex-pro. **Tomás Domingo** is another big road-bike shop, with two locations in the city, one in the centre and one in the Sant Gervasi neighbourhood to the north. The **Orbea Bicicletas** flagship store has a small but good selection of racing stuff, and is the place to pick up your Euskaltel replica jersey (the brand has sponsored the de facto Basque 'national' team since day one) and to chat with Sisquillo the mechanic, who, having wrenched for the likes of Eddy Merckx, Mario Cipollini and Oscar Freire, is a local living

legend. **Green Bikes** is a trustworthy place to get your bike fixed, and they'll also rent you a road bike if you need one; for more bike-hire options, see Essential Bike Info (p. 40). And, finally, for some high-end bike porn in a setting more akin to an art gallery, **Pavé** is the place; it's located a few kilometres south of the city in El Prat de Llobregat.

The Catalans aren't as racing crazy as their western cousins, the Basques, but there's still a strong road-racing culture here. The **Volta a Catalunya** stage race, one of the key early season fixtures, always finishes in Barcelona. In 2013 it was won by Garmin-Sharp's Dan Martin, who as a Girona resident counted it a 'home' victory. As for real locals, Joaquim 'Purito' Rodríguez honed his explosive style in nearby Parets del Vallès, while the late Xavier Tondo was originally from Valls, 90km (56 miles) west of Barcelona. Spain's first-ever yellow-jersey wearer, Miguel Poblet, who died in 2013, was from Montcada i Reixac, a Barcelona suburb. In 1955 Poblet, a Tour de France debutant, won the first stage from Le Havre to Dieppe for the Spanish national team and held it for the afternoon's team time trial, before losing it the next day. Surprisingly, the Tour has visited Barcelona only three times. The last time, in 2009, Thor Hushovd won the stage, surviving the climb to the **Estadi Olímpic Lluís Companys** (p. 18), on his way to winning the overall-points jersey that year. The **Vuelta Ciclista a España**, meanwhile, had not been to the Catalan capital for thirteen years before 2012, as the organizers had historically avoided the north for fear of separatist terrorism. That stage was won by the Belgian Philippe Gilbert, again at the Olympic stadium.

It seems the climb to Montjuïc has always been attractive to cyclists: until 2007, the Escalada a Montjuïc was one of the closing race fixtures of the professional season. It comprised a criterium in the city streets in the morning and a hill-climb in the afternoon, and was won six times by Eddy Merckx. Learn more about Montjuïc and the Olympics in our Montjuïc chapter (p. 16), but for now, here's one final Olympic thought: the 1992 Games was where Chris Boardman, aboard a futuristic carbon Lotus bike, won the 4,000m individual pursuit, claiming Britain's first cycling gold for seventy-two years. Many attribute the British track squad's dominance in the 2000s to his inspiring performance.

ESSENTIAL BIKE INFO

Locals and tourists alike have ball cycling around Barcelona. Here are some tips to keep you rolling.

ETIQUETTE

There aren't loads of cyclists on Barcelona's roads, and it's very laid back, but there are some things you should look out for:

- If a cycle lane is on the pavement, you must give priority to pedestrians crossing it. If, however, it's on the road, you have the same status as other traffic.
- Pavement cycling seems to be OK with Barcelonans, but be respectful, slow and sensible.
- Likewise, in the many shared-use, car-free streets in the old town, be really courteous to the crowds of people walking.

SAFETY

Barcelona is not over-endowed with bike lanes, but much of the old town is virtually traffic-free, and the faster roads are well covered. Here's some more safety advice:

- Car drivers seem mostly courteous, but roads can be narrow, so keep your wits about you.
- Work out where the bike lanes are and take them. Some roads, such as Gran Via de les Corts Catalanes and Carrer d'Aragó, are four lanes wide, but the parallel street has a bike path that will take you exactly where you need to go.
- Keep an eye out while in and around La Rambla or any other party zones for glass in the road, particularly after a Saturday night.
- Some of the rental places literally cannot change a puncture. Check your bike's roadworthiness carefully when you rent.

SECURITY

Barcelona has a bigger problem than some cities with bicycle theft, especially in the old town. Your hire bike should come with a chain lock, and we recommend using it to tie the bike to something immovable if you're going to leave it unattended. Do not leave any bike unlocked and unattended, and take your cues from local cyclists: if you don't see any bikes locked in a certain area, then it's probably not a good idea to leave yours there either. In the centre of town it can be difficult to find a railing or bike stand to lock to, but it's a good idea to do so, and, if you've come to town with a valuable bike, it's essential. Think about using two locks, and securing the wheels, so that opportunist bike thieves will pick an easier target.

FINDING YOUR WAY

Barcelona's coastline, which runs diagonally from southwest to northeast, is a good reference point, and makes the city easy to navigate. If you head inland, the grid of streets in L'Eixample and Poblenou is easy to understand, and, although Gràcia and Poble Sec are a maze of small streets, the rising ground often gives you views over the city that can help you orient yourself. The system of road signs leaves a lot to be desired, but the Metro stops are good landmarks.

CITY BIKES AND BIKE HIRE

Bicing, the city's bike-sharing scheme, is not open to non-residents, which is a real shame. It seems the existing bike-hire places in the city ganged up to protect their interests and imposed this rule on the city council when it proposed the scheme, meaning that visitors are effectively barred from using part of Barcelona's public transport system – and the most fun, environmentally friendly part at that. It goes to show that bike rental in Barcelona is big business, and even though the Bicing bikes are not for tourists, you won't have trouble finding a bike. Some places hire only brightly coloured bikes, others inconspicuous, black step-through models; one bike-hire place we encountered could not repair a flat tyre, so take a good look at a shop's stock of machines before you commit to hiring, as maintenance standards can vary.

We recommend **Green Bikes** (p. 39) for a good reliable city bike. For something more stylish, try **Barceloneta Bikes** or **My Beautiful Parking**, which has a rental place in <u>Carrer dels Vigatans</u>, close to its Born boutique. For an electric bike, try **e-Bike Rent** or **Freeel**, which has rental points in the city. For a road bike, try Green Bikes or **Terra Diversions**, which also rents mountain bikes.

OTHER PUBLIC TRANSPORT

Bikes are not allowed on the city's buses. You can, however, take your bike on the Metro, but not between 7 and 9:30am, or 5 and 8:30pm on working days. Weekends and public holidays are OK.

Renfe is the main train operator in Spain. You can take a bike on its local Cercanias (also known as Rodalies) trains, in the designated space if there is one, or otherwise in the space by the doors.

Bikes are not allowed on cable cars, including the **Transbordador Aeri del Port**, which crosses the Port of Barcelona, and the **Telefèric de Montjuïc**, which takes passengers up to the Castell de Montjuïc (p. 17).

TRAVELLING TO BARCELONA WITH BIKES

Barcelona is the first major stop on international trains from France, so it is well served by fast trains. There are no bicycles allowed on Spain's high-speed trains, but put your bike in a bag and it's welcomed. The same goes for French trains travelling across the border: bicycles are usually fine on slower services, but you'll need to put it in a bag if you're travelling on a TGV. The large luggage racks mean the whole business is fairly hassle-free, and two strategies seem to work: either race to the front of the queue, so that you can be sure of securing the space you want in the rack; or, if your bike bag is fairly slimline, wait until everyone else has stowed their luggage, and slide it in on top.

The Regional Exprés trains, which tend to be stopping services, usually allow bikes, and without a bike ticket bought in advance. There is a designated bicycle section at the front of the trains, but if this is full, the conductors will usually tolerate bikes in the corridors. On the longer-range Media Distancia trains, you have to obtain a (free) bike ticket before getting on. They have space for three bikes, and these are rarely full; if they are full, and you have a ticket, again you should be OK with the conductor.

Unfortunately, if you're travelling from Britain, **Eurostar** will not, from 2013, allow a bagged bike as normal carry-on luggage. The maximum baggage dimensions are 85 × 85cm (33 × 33 in.), which rules out all but folding bikes. Instead, you must either book your bike a place (currently £30 per journey; it will be hung on a hook in the goods van), or put it in a bag and send it via the registered baggage service.

If you're going to send your bike as registered baggage, the 'Turn Up and Go' option, where you leave your bike bag at a counter in the check-in hall, costs £10 each way, and although Eurostar believes it will meet demand, you're not 100 per cent guaranteed it will travel on the same train as you. If you have a tight connection and need to guarantee your bike is with you, book in advance through Eurostar's freight service. If you do this, make sure you arrive in good time at the station: the registered baggage counter is quite a walk from the departure gates. It's possible these regulations will change, so do check the Eurostar website for the most up-to-date information.

Barcelona Airport is down the coast in El Prat de Llobregat. It's close to the centre of town, but surrounded by industrial estates and fast roads – it's probably best to keep your bike in its box and take the Metro into town.

LINKS AND ADDRESSES

Alzira
Carrer de Verdi, 42, 08012
mueblesalzira.com

Antic Convent de Sant Agustí
Carrer del Comerç, 36, 08003

Arts Santa Mònica
La Rambla, 7, 08002
artssantamonica.cat

Barcelona Digital Centro Tecnológico
Carrer de Roc Boronat, 117, 08018
bdigital.org

Bar Pastis
Carrer de Santa Mònica, 4, 08001
barpastis.com

Bar Seco
Passeig del Montjuïc, 74,
Cantonada Nou de la Rambla, 08004
barseco.blogspot.com

BD Barcelona Design
Carrer de Ramon Turró, 126, 08005
bdbarcelona.com

Belvedere
Passatge de Mercader, 3, 08008

Betty Ford
Carrer de Joaquín Costa, 56, 08001

Bobby Gin
Carrer de Francisco Giner, 47, 08012
bobbygin.com

Bohèmic
Carrer de Manso, 42, 08015

Botafumeiro
Carrer Gran de Gràcia, 81, 08012
botafumeiro.es

CaixaForum
Av. Francesc Ferrer i Guàrdia, 6–8, 08038
obrasocial.lacaixa.es

Can Framis
Carrer de Roc Boronat, 116–126, 08018

Caravelle
Carrer Pintor Fortuny, 31, 08001

Casa Amatller
Passeig de Gràcia, 41, 08007
amatller.com

Casa Batlló
Passeig de Gràcia, 43, 08007
casabatllo.es

Casa Camper
Carrer d'Elisabets, 11, 08001
casacamper.com

Casa Comalat
Av. Diagonal, 442, 08036

Casa Milà
Carrer Provença, 261, 08008
lapedrera.com

Casa Vicens
Carrer Carolines, 18, 08012
casavicens.es

Caseta del Migdia
Carrer del Molí, 08038
lacaseta.org

Castell de Montjuïc
Carretera de Montjuïc, 66, 08038
castillomontjuic.com

CCCB
Montalegre, 5, 08001
cccb.org

Cementiri de Montjuïc
Carrer de la Mare de Déu de Port, 56, 08038
cbsa.es

Cementiri de Poblenou
Av. Icària, s/n, 08005
cbsa.es

Chandal
Carrer de Valldonzella, 29, 08001
shop.chandal.tv

Chiringuito Inercia
Playa de Nova Icària, 08005

Chiringuito Mochima
Playa la Mar Bella, s/n, 08005
chiringuitoben.com

Churrería El Trébol
Carrer de Còrsega, 341, 08037

Cosmo
Carrer Enric Granados, 3, 08007
galeriacosmo.com

Discos Paradiso
Ferlandina, 39, 08001
discosparadiso.com

Dos Palillos
Carrer d'Elisabets, 9, 08001
dospalillos.com

Duduá
Carrer del Diluvi, 5, 08012
duduadudua.com

El Ciclista
Carrer de Mozart, 18, 08012

El Magnífico
Carrer de l'Argenteria, 64, 08003
cafeselmagnifico.com

El Quim de la Boqueria
Mercado de La Boqueria,
La Rambla, 91, 08002
elquimdelaboqueria.com

Els Encants
Plaça de les Glories Catalanes, 08018
encantsbcn.com

Els Jardinets de Gràcia
Passeig de Gràcia, 116, 08008
elsjardinetsdegracia.com

Els Pescadors
Plaça de Prim, 1, 08005
elspescadors.com

El Velódromo
Carrer Muntaner, 213, 08036

Fàbrica Moritz
Ronda de Sant Antoni, 41, 08011
moritz.com

Filmoteca de Catalunya
Plaça Salvador Seguí, 1, 08001
filmoteca.cat

Forn Baluard
Carrer del Baluart, 38, 08003
baluardbarceloneta.com

Fundació Antoni Tàpies
Carrer d'Aragó, 255, 08007
fundaciotapies.org

Fundació Joan Miró
Parc de Montjuïc, s/n, 08038
fundaciomiro-bcn.org

Fundació Palo Alto
Carrer dels Pellaires, 30–38, 08019
paloaltobcn.org

Gelateria Italiana
Plaça de la Revolució de Setembre de 1868, 2, 08012

Grey Street
Calle Peu de la Creu, 25, 08001

Heliogàbal
Carrer de Ramón y Cajal, 80, 08012
heliogabal.com

Hotel Barceló Raval
Rambla del Raval, 17–21, 08001
barcelo.com

Hotel ME Barcelona
Carrer Pere IV, 272, 08005
melia.com

Ikastola
La Perla, 22, 08012

Ivo & Co
Carrer del Rec, 20, 08003
ivoandco.com

Jai-Ca
Carrer Ginebra, 13, 08003

Jardí Botànic
Carrer del Doctor Font i Quer,
2, 08038
jardibotanic.bcn.cat

Kiosko
Av. del Marquès de l'Argentera,
1 bis, 08003
kioskoburger.com

Kowasa
Carrer de Mallorca, 235, 08008
kowasa.com

La Boqueria
Carrer de la Boqueria, 08002
boqueria.info

La Fibula
Carrer Blai, 46, 08004

La Fourmi
Carrer de l'Alba, 2, 08012

L'Appartement
Carrer d'Enric Granados, 44
08008
lappartement.es

La Taqueria
Passatge Font, 5, 08013

La Tomaquera
Carrer de Margarit, 58, 08004

Lletraferit
Carrer de Joaquín Costa, 43,
08011

Llibreria La Central del Raval
Carrer d'Elisabets, 6, 08001
lacentral.com

Los Juanele
Carrer d'Aldana, 4, 08015

L'Ovella Negra
Carrer de Zamora 78, 08018
ovellanegra.com

Luchador Records
Ferlandina, 39 derecha, 08001
luchadorrecords.tumblr.com

MACBA
Plaça dels Àngels, 1, 08001
macba.cat

Marsella
Carrer de Sant Pau, 65, 08001

Mercat de la Concepció
Carrer d'Aragó, 313–317, 08009
laconcepcio.com

Mercat de les Flors
Carrer Lleida, 59, 08004
mercatflors.cat

MIBA
Carrer de la Ciutat, 7, 08002
mibamuseum.com

Mirablau
Carrer de Manuel Arnús, 2,
08035

Miscelànea
Calle Guardia, 10, 08001
miscelanea.info

MNAC
Palau Nacional, Parc de
Montjuïc, s/n, 08038
mnac.cat

Monvínic
Carrer de la Diputació, 249,
08007
monvinic.com

Museu Blau
Parque del Fórum, Plaza
Leonardo da Vinci, 4–5, 08019
museublau.bcn.cat

**Museu Olímpic i de l'Esport
Joan Antoni Samaranch**
Av. de l'Estadi, 60, 08038
museuolimpicbcn.cat

Museu Picasso
Carrer Montcada, 15–23, 08003
museupicasso.bcn.cat

Mutt
Carrer del Comerç, 15, 08003
mutt.es

Niu BCN
Carrer dels Almogàvers, 208,
08018
niubcn.com

Olivia Cafè
Carrer Pintor Fortuny, 22, 08001

Palau Baró de Quadras
Av. Diagonal, 373, 08008

Parc de la Ciutadella
Passeig de Picasso, 21, 08018

Parc del Centre del Poblenou
Av. Diagonal, 130, 08018

Parc de la Diagonal Mar
Carrer de Llull, 08019
barcelonaturisme.com/
parc-diagonal-mar

Parc del Fòrum
Rambla de Prim, 1, 08019

Parc Güell
Carrer d'Olot 5, 08024
parkguell.es

Parc Joan Miró
Carrer d'Aragó, 2, 08015

Pavelló Mies van der Rohe
Av. Francesc Ferrer i Guàrdia,
7, 08038
miesbcn.com

Piscina Municipal de Montjuïc
Avinguda de Miramar, 0, 08038

Quimet & Quimet
Carrer del Poeta Cabanyes,
25, 08004

Razzmatazz
Carrer Almogàvers, 122, 08018
salarazzmatazz.com

Roca
Av. Diagonal, 513, 080298
roca.es

Sagrada Família
Calle Mallorca, 401, 08013
sagradafamilia.cat

Sagrat Cor
Cumbre del Tibidabo, s/n,
08035
templotibidabo.info

Santa Eulalia
Passeig de Gràcia, 93, 08008
santaeulalia.com

Santa Marta
Carrer de Grau i Torras, 59,
08003

Satan's Coffee Corner
Carrer Peu de la Creu, 25, 08001

Sésamo
Carrer de Sant Antoni Abat,
52, 08001

Sidecar
Plaça Reial, 7, 08002
sidecarfactoryclub.com

Sol Soler
Plaça del Sol, 21, 08012

Sombrerería Obach
Carrer del Call, 2, 08002
barretsobach.com

Telefèric de Montjuïc
tmb.cat

The Outpost
Carrer Rosselló, 281, 08037
theoutpostbcn.com

Tinto Roja
Carrer de la Creu dels Molers,
17, 08004
tintoroja.cat

Torre Agbar
Av. Diagonal, 211, 08018
agbar.es

Torre d'Alta Mar
Passeig de Joan de Borbó, 88,
08023
torredealtamar.com

Torre de Collserola
Carretera de Vallvidrera al
Tibidabo, 08017
torredecollserola.com

Transbordador Aeri del Port
Carretera de Vallvidrera al
Tibidabo, 08017
portvellbcn.com

Viblioteca
Carrer Vallfogona, 12, 08012
viblioteca.com

Vinçon
Passeig de Gràcia, 96, 08008
vincon.com

W Barcelona
Plaça Rosa dels Vents, 1, 08039
w-barcelona.com

Wilde Vintage
• Carrer de Joaquín Costa, 2,
08001
• Carrer de Avinyó, 21, 08002
wildestore.com

Zodiaco
Carrer Comte d'Urgell, 22, 08011

BIKE SHOPS, CLUBS, RACES AND VENUES

For links to our racing and
training routes, please visit
citycyclingguides.com

Barceloneta Bikes
Carrer de l'Atlàntida, 49, 08003
barcelonetabikes.com

Bicing
bicing.cat

CC Gràcia
Carrer de Sant Pere Màrtir,
16, 08012
ccgracia.org

e-Bike Rent
Carrer Cervantes 5, 08002
e-bikerent.com

EC Sant Andreu
Carrer Gran de Sant Andreu,
111, 08030
ecsantandreu.com

**Estadi Olímpic Lluís
Companys**
Av. de l'Estadi, 60, 08038

Freeel
Carrer Ros de Olano 11, 08012
freeel.org

Galvesport
Carrer de la Diputació, 69, 08015

Green Bikes
Carrer dels Escudellers, 48,
08002
greenbikesbarcelona.com

My Beautiful Parking
Carrer dels Vigatans, 2, 08003
mybeautifulparking.com

Orbea Bicicletas
Carrer Gran de Gràcia, 1, 08012
orbea.com

Pavé
Carrer Alcalde Ferrer i Monés,
57–59, 08820 El Prat del
Llobregat
pave.cc

Rocacorba
bikecat.com/rocacorba

Terra Diversions
Carrer Santa Tecla, 1, 08012
terradiversions.com

Tomás Domingo
• Carrer Sepúlveda, 109, 08015
• Paseo Sant Gervasi 12, 08015
tomasdomingo.com

Volta a Catalunya
voltacatalunya.cat

Vuelta Ciclista a España
lavuelta.com

OTHER USEFUL SITES

Barcelona Airport
08820 Prat de Llobregat
barcelona-airport.com

Estació de Sant Andreu Arenal
Avenida Meridiana con Fabra i
Puig, 08030
transportebcn.es

Eurostar
eurostar.com

Renfe
renfe.com

Rapha, established in London, has always been a champion of city cycling – from testing our first prototype jackets on the backs of bike couriers, to a whole range of products designed specifically for the demands of daily life on the bike. As well as an online emporium of products, films, photography and stories, Rapha has a growing network of Cycle Clubs, locations around the globe where cyclists can enjoy live racing, food, drink and products. Rapha is also the official clothing supplier of Team Sky, the world's leading cycling team.

Rapha.